How to Tie Tobacco

Poetry by:

A.M. HAYDEN

CAMP HILL, PENNSYLVANIA

A.M. Hayden's How to Tie Tobacco brings the history of women's work to life in a sensory way, through exact images: handmade blankets, butterbeans, and washboards. We travel with Hayden to the tobacco farming South of her grandmothers. It is a gift and a stab to the heart to experience so precisely, through the living language of these extraordinarily crafted poems and the ephemera of artifact photographs and snippets of handwriting, the reality of being a woman tasked with raising the next generation of women, often under a looming shadow of constriction or control. This collection feels sacredly passed down, like a secret recipe or a home remedy. In the end, it is more than an "attempt to breathe what's frozen," more than a reminder that women "fit for the devil" can't help but "hurt our mothers," it is a "love letter," a "promise" to waste nothing. It is a reminder that we all carry history in us, and we fiercely survive it.

- **Sara Moore Wagner**, Poet and Managing Poetry Editor of Driftwood Press, Author of Lady Wing Shot, Swan Wife, and Hillbilly Madonna

In How to Tie Tobacco, A. M. Hayden's poetry sings like the winds rustling through the leaves of the south and in the holler, extolling the virtues and simple dignity of the folk she portrays with fondness; a potent antidote to so many other contemporary depictions of Southern and Appalachian women. This is a love letter to multiple generations of "ma-mas."

- **J. R. Simons**, Publisher, Simple Simons Press

The photos and poems say one thing: authentic. Each poem speaks its own truth while bringing the voice of the collection together. The past has its way of showing itself in the present...anchoring us when the present seems difficult, reminding us of our strength. We have the ability to overcome, leaning on history to propel us forward. Hayden's poetic voice is one that honors the past while moving forward with a beaming hope reminding us that we can honor what was and honor what can be.

- **Jason Blakely**, Poet/ Publisher, Poetry Is Life Publishing

In How to Tie Tobacco, we step into the heart of home to thread staunch, taut strings around the tender truths and stubbornness that live there. Intimate lines, arresting justifications, and visual poetic devices, guide us through this stunning debut chapbook as the author presses hands with ancestors in dream and form, paying tribute to the resolve of womanhood and lineage from age to age. Honoring joy and loss, Hayden reaches across each familial abyss, diving into the invisibly treacherous waters women have always been made to navigate. Stoic faces buried in busywork look up from the page to share their wisdom asking that circles hold fast and patterns be broken.

- **Holly Brians Ragusa**, Author of Met the End, Inverse, and Tilt a World, President of Ohio Poetry Association

How to Tie Tobacco

A.M. HAYDEN

Wild Ink Publishing

A Wild Ink Publishing Original
wild-ink-publishing.com

Copyright © 2025 A.M. Hayden
Edited by Brittany McMunn
Cover Design and Layout by Abigail Wild
Cover photo courtesy of the A.M. Hayden family archives

ISBN: 978-1-964885-18-6

For Virginia, Hannah, Lena Lura, Selma, Kakie,
Wendy, Brenda, Starr, Judy, Alice Rainwater,
Aunt Laura, and the other women whom I never met,
who live in my imagination and in my palms, and my
daughters, who carry on their blueprints and songs

All photos/images/notes from the
Hayden/Thompson/Bellamy family archive with
permission or by the author

Table of Contents

Credits

Bless their hearts and a heap of gratitude to the editors who first published these individual poems:

Snuff Clouds in South Carolina, *30 Poets in 30 Days*, 2023; *Flights Literary Magazine*, 2024; *American Saunter: Poems of the U.S.*, FlowerSong Press, 2024
Caretaker Covenant, *Etymology Press*, 2024
Holy Waters, *Freshwater Review*, 2024
We all Hurt our Mother at some Point, *Silver Birch Press*, 2024
Look 'em, *Locust Shells Journal*, 2024
Egg Exchange, *When the River Speaks*, 2024
Forgive Them, *Flora Fiction*, 2025
Kitchen Cures, *Voices of Real, Poetry is Life*, 2025
Love Letter to my Grandmothers, *Tangled Locks Journal*, 2025

Cheesecake Pg
Fresh applesauce cake
Corn fondue
Pecan Pie
Egg nog

My mama always said,
"A whistling woman
and a crowing hen
is both fit for the devil,
but not for the men."

Look 'em

Today you are a secret keeper
because you don't eat pork
so, you pretend to not hear
how she conjured these dripping
silk collards, greased them
with fatback slabs, soaked them
in hog jowl, after she first doused
the leaves in cool sink water to look 'em
for bugs, worms, and other garden critters
and so, you tune out all that jowl and slab
take spoonfuls of sliding butterbeans,
penny-sized black-eyed peas, sop up
all the fixins with a flaky buttery biscuit
because she put her foot in this food
and anyone who doubts a southern
woman needs only watch her raw cut
the green leaves, squeezed tight in one fist,
with the serrated knife in the other
suspended straight in the air
striking like a copperhead
without hesitation

HOW TO TIE TOBACCO

We all Hurt our Mother at Some Point

Step out, the sun will do the rest, it's hard to walk

On ground plowed or bumpy with plums or pears

A woodfired cookstove, echo of his pendulum clock

Crack the shell against mixing bowl into sweet milk

Break apart, stripped peach tree leaves fall to pieces

Your wild laughter bubbles up the washboard, your

Mother's rub tub, avocado wash bowl, and sea island
pitcher take me

Back to crisp muslin sheets, color of sand, apricots
sun-blushed, sweet tea in June's breeze

HOW TO TIE TOBACCO

Snuff Clouds in South Carolina

Southern Baptist Jesus hung in the hallway
she smelled of Irish spring and fresh powder
fleshy arms, clean and soft as baby legs, hands
rolled biscuits in the army bowl, hands cooked collard greens
and boiled peanuts from the Piggly Wiggly, "the Pig" she called
it, hands dried and tied tobacco from the fields, snapped string
beans under pine trees until worn slap out, hands dipped peach
snuff, powdery brown clouds, lingered from each laugh
as she passed gas in morse code wall to wall of her
chicken fried kitchen, hands stirred paper thin aprons,
handkerchiefs, and stiff shirts with a long wooden stick in the
blackened cast iron cauldron her granddaughter's hands now fill
each May with purple petunias and yellow marigolds
petals pour over like holy water
Lord have mercy

Horry County Zen Garden

The story goes like this
    front yards had no grass then
        just dirt, and mounds of it

the young' ins were taught to rake
    the clay into neat, even rows, just so
        before each Sunday morning

the brother, who had polio at age five, before sugar
    cubes dropped onto lined up tongues,
        surveyed from porch rocking chair

the sister, eyes squinted, gripped handle, leveled
    their little piece of earth into perfectly
        pointed arrows standing at attention

when she completed the last row, she forearm wiped
    her brow, put her other hand on her hip,
        beheld her satisfying succession

the brother shuffled down the stoop and hollered,
    "The Yankees are coming!" limp leg lagging
        each step, dead into her plumb lines

a released oar off the side of a canoe
    he dragged his limb straight through all her
        precision, obstinate obliteration

she cried and ran to her Mama,
   "he did it on purpose!"
     fists curled tight, foot stomping

he clasped his hands behind his back
   insisting, as he always did… "but I had polio"
    smirk slowly spreading his lips

*Horry is pronounced "Orry."

The General

It was December when she lined every cigar can in formation,
silver paper labels all facing out, reckoned she needn't make
a fuss needn't tell him how much he smoked,
how much he spent of their cash this year, the row
would command his gaze as he walked to the kitchen
and paused, eyeing the neatly stacked cylinders, one end
to other, back in the living room he found her kneeling catty-
wampus in front of the Christmas tree, knee caps pestles
for shed sharp needles, hands carefully wrapping walnuts,
hickory nuts, small egg-shaped pine cones, swaddling each one
with the soft silver cigar paper, silk peeled gingerly
from each can, her crinkled eyes betraying a tight smirk
reflected in every hanging tinsel pouch

>   spinning mirror ball
>   shining glittered ornament
>   brazen between bulbs

*The sentence is an organism, of which
the soul is the thought, and the body the word.*

HOW TO TIE TOBACCO

Egg Exchange

She was fourteen the day her mom fetched her
run next door to Jerry's folks for butter and eggs
she knocked three times until the door opened
Jerry stood there as she made the request
he glanced at her, then pointed at the bed
in the adjacent room, his silent proposed barter
wedged in her chest, choked her like cigar smoke
she spun around and sprinted down
each porch step, holding her britches up tight
and didn't stop running
until she plowed through her front door
where she paused, out of breath, and lied
to her Mama for the first time,
They were out, Daddy'll have to carry you to town.

Party Line

Nosy Rosie, the widowed neighbor
sat on her porch among her hydrangeas

chickens clucking in her garden beds
each Sunday, she'd snatch one by its head

boil and pluck and take it by its rough leg
dangle the bird upside down over gas flame

pendulum singe to fowl fuzz and bumpy skin
worn ritual to morning's hymns atoning sins

besides her hens, Rosie had a highfalutin phone line
she shared with three other neighbors nearby

she would hush her kettle's mouth from whistling
then sit to lift her banana yellow receiver, listening

quiet and careful to heed any revealing and hearsay
a good Christian woman listened every *other* day

spent good lazy afternoons unraveling their thread
ear pressed for years until the day she was dead

(Pivotal words,) In all sentences there are
what we might call "pivotal words," on
which the meaning of a sentence rests.

Haystack Hominy

he photographs her
pressed into golden dome
both chafing her like coarse grits

Dead Ringer Villanelle

She saw it with her own two eyes
      at the First Baptist church in town
all the bun ladies gasped and fell out
      pocketbooks hit the floor
when Willie sat straight up in his casket,
      shocked eyes gazing around

even though doc's stethoscope
      picked up no sound
it was a stir when he climbed out of his coffin
      and headed for the door
She saw it with her own two eyes
      at the First Baptist church in town

They knew then a different kind
      of method must be found
to ensure this would not occur again
      for Willie lived six months more
after he sat up in his casket,
      shocked eyes gazing around

from then on, they tied a bell
      to a string through the burial mound
someone enlisted to sit graveside and listen
      a job that made most bored
She saw it with her own two eyes
      at the First Baptist church in town

For in the rare chance, they were only *mostly* dead,
       this peace of mind was profound
"I was at your funeral, Bubba!"
       became repeated refrain of town lore
after Willie sat straight up in his casket,
       shocked eyes gazing around

His last request if he died again: to roll him down
       the church steps 'til he smacked the ground
Willie made them promise to push him three times
       over, to make certain he was no more
She saw it all with her own two eyes
       at the First Baptist church in town
when Willie sat straight up in his casket,
       shocked eyes gazing around

The Ghosts of Terrible Things

Miss Mary Mack Mack Mack
       never left the laundry turned inside out
cradled heads of the dying in her lap

all dressed in black, black, black
       used every part of everything
hand "warshed" clothes in lye

reached to the sky, sky, sky
       she says, we've come a long way
but there's a long way to go, by and by

and that's no lie, lie, lie
       packed his lunch in a shoebox tied
in tobacco twine, mended, and sewed

big silver buttons, buttons, buttons
       remembers granny grinding the corn
carries heart troubles and the sins of these men

down her back, back, back
       a tree, when attacked, forms burls and knots
bark swells like a pufferfish to protect itself

to heal the damage done, done, done
       from those who got religion and those who
never did, and those who trespass against us

References:
Miss Mary Mack – hand clapping children's rhyme, documented in The Counting Out Rhymes of Children, Henry Carrington Bolton, 1888.
"ghosts of terrible things" from Wild and Precious: A Celebration of Mary Oliver, Pushkin Industries, 2024.

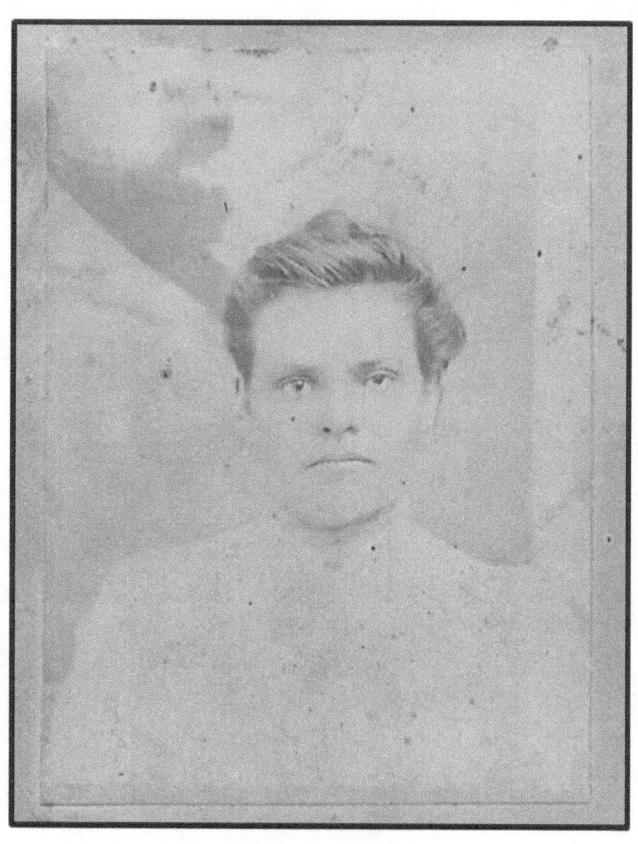

Broom Cookies

She liked to dance the Jitterbug, the Charleston
       and hide her favorite cookies from her son

one night, a squirrel dropped down her chimney
       bounced into her house, straight into her bed

where she lay, glasses off, her screams and stomps
       could instantly be heard across the house

"A rat is in bed with me!" she shrieked
       broom smacking the bedsheets

the son ran in and lifted the blankets
       to see a tiny fur form, flat as a postcard

"It's a squirrel, Mama, not a rat," he said
       "Lord, no matter, it had no business in my bed"

then he noticed a second broom casualty,
       her bedside table knocked over on its side

his eyes followed the crumbled trail from its drawer
       his favorite cookies sprinkled over oak floor

Judy, I bought this butter dish the day I was married, we walked through a dime store and I picked this up, have took good care of it and I want you to have it, There was only round butter in those days no stick one then, Keep in mind I love you all, ma-ma

The Visit

The first night of the family reunion, I dreamed my great-grand-mother sat down in front of me, folded my hands in hers, held my gaze, and declared, "I'm so happy y'all getting together like this. I'm just tickled to see all these young'ins running around." Her voice was raspy, just as I remember, her face soft and full of whiskers, inches from mine. When I woke, I went to find my mother in the kitchen. "I just dreamed of Ma-Ma, she was happy we are all here together." Mom turned from the sink, coffee mug in hand, eyes widened, "She came to me last night too."

Family Tree

CW: Maternal loss

fingertips follow each line and date, past the twins
who passed from malaria three weeks apart,
then three more, *Infant, Aug 1944, b.d.* same day
just below, again, *Infant, July 1945, b.d.* same day
catch of breath

the next line has a name, Frankie, *b. Aug 1946*
 d…Feb 1947, seven months on this side, and my
fingers drop away, was it separate underwater
hollows for this mother, resurfacing in between,
or her personal Mariana trench

plummeting down sunless existence, deeper into
gaping abyss of grief, the place itself formidable
fractures, scars across ocean floor, chasm
of her hearts chamber each time her arms emptied
with a *Hades zone* for christsakes

unbearable milkiness, somehow still breathing
clinging to whatever can be gripped in lament's
void, squeezed freezing pressure, stolen lives
in purgatory, unlived family branches buried
behind silent walls

too arcane to hear distant calls, biologists
asked for decades whether life could exist
in this greatest inhospitable depth, and they discovered,
yes, it could, but must affix aluminum shell
over translucent body, a slippery

biolumenscent cloak, a newly formed ability to digest
the undigestable, to spit out placation
and pity in the furthest space from surface sounds
nothing left except an attempt to breathe
what's frozen, what eternally exists in oblivion

Holy Waters

You always plant in rows, dig little holes with the long-handled
scoop, drop soft baby plant

its tiny bulb of earth holding on, every row, every hole, this
takes time, then imbue with water

It was this well where he tried to drown his three-year-old
sister, took her by the leg and held

her upside down as she shrieked and cried, her arms flapped
and flew over water

her Gullah Geechee family friend helped deliver the children,
all six born in that old yellow house

no electricity or running faucets, buckets gathered in boil, each
wet sac induced with water

in the black cauldron, she used lard, and a raw cut tobacco
stick to poke and agitate

the wash until liquid turned brown, then twisted, wrung, and
rinsed through lucid water

she always said, to reverse the bad luck of a broken mirror,
immediately immerse

the shards into a river, under a faucet, or running bath, as long
as it's flowing, moving water

while the rich ladies buy their silver rice charms, you cook the
bog, broth, chicken thighs, pork, or turkey

but what made it *bog* was buckets of Waccamaw river, stewed
with water

stretch the hose yonder to the garden, douse the soil under the
ripe tomatoes and myrtle trees

early in the morning, set its rusted mouth just under the
leaves, dewed with water

braided buns and hands on scripture, opened hymnals and holy spirit sermons

old rugged cross, on and off the pew, flood and dunk baptism, renewed with water

and the day she went from wife to widow, the women gathered in her living room

sat her down, placed a bucket at her knees,
soaked her feet in warm, soothing water

Lightnin' Rules

If you hear thunder
you best lift them feet up and keep 'em lifted
don't touch that carpet

Kitchen Cures

A glass jar black with lamp coal oil
molasses thick for a swollen finger
slammed in a heavy front door

A cottonball full of warm
melted butter stuck in your ear
to ease an earache

A teaspoon of paregoric
honey licorice tincture anytime for a stomachache flowers
of Benjamin and notes of opium make the pain go away

A finger rub of whiskey
to hush baby's tender teething gums
soothing for everyone

A shot of whiskey and spoonful of honey for a cold
A pinch of homemade headache powder
dumped in your mouth like a pixie stick

A freezer full of homemade pies
pecans from out back, eggs from yardbirds
you never know when someone will drop by

Caretaker Covenant

I don't know what to do, she cried
after he fell and broke his hip, refused
to see the doctor, before she became his reluctant
nurse, she fed and fixed goats, handwrote tea
postcards, fashioned quilts for future grandbabies
she was born with a stained-glass heart
that had carried her lifetime of unbroken covenants
pumped a prohibitionist's passion, a pilgrim's piety
she begged him to get help, instead, he hissed her
through blurred weeks, she spread her homemade
blanket down for him to sit, to drag his limp
bones and heavy heart across the living room floor
to the bathroom tile, back and forth shuffle
each day until the afternoon her prism heart shattered,
she fainted and fell to the floor
pillar of salt and light, silence cradled
in her chest, and he crawled
to the phone, picked up the receiver
and cried, *I don't know what to do*
as it rang and rang

Every day from April to August.
25 cents an hour.

How to Tie Tobacco

(top and crop) it's ready when they start lookin' like tall green corn-stalks, puffy tufts out the top like some Dr. Seuss book. Start with topping all those puffs from the get-go. Get your wagon and a mule. Hire four teenaged boys as croppers, they'll drag along the beds, leaves like big elephant ears, 30-40 or so on each stalk, they'll crop 'em until their wagon's overfilling and carry to the barn where the women and children fix to do the tying.

(tie) pile all cropped leaves on the wide block bench, gather the rough-cut tobacco sticks, those four-footers them youngins have been galloping around with playing horse. Bring three big leaves together, stems lined up, like them Irish clovers, tie a good knot, tie each bundle to a stick, one after another down the line, until there's no stick left. Now, if you're a *really* good stringer, which I *was*, you whipped that stick out mighty quick, cleared that shelf clean empty in no time, and before you know it, those boys come back, another wagon heaving, each time, their rough hands blacker, leaf-stained, their hair wet and plastered across their freckled foreheads lookin' like wilted seagrass. But there is no time to dawdle for them, you got to start hanging each stringed stick from those long barn rafters until they are filled, all draping down like Spanish moss from tree branches.

(break) dinner is at noon, always fresh, fried chicken still popping grease like a cat on a hot tin roof, churned potatoes, collards melting on your tongue, buttery cobcorn, you, kids, croppers, doesn't matter, you all take your dinner and a cold coke, sit in the shade of the pine trees.

(cure) after sunset, the exhausted croppers have gone back home in pickups, now, the real work begins as you light the fire inside the barn, get it to just the right temperature. You become the fire tender, for about 3 or 4 days. It takes time to get it right and everything's on you to make sure to keep it delicate, somewhere between green and brown, pliable but not soft, crisp, but not crispy. Like a midwife, you're just the guide through the earthy and sweet-smelling burn, with a lot of waiting and monitoring, which can feel like a coon's age. You can't leave it for a second, so you just move that big bench outside the barn under lean to each night, drape a big quilt, curl yourself up on top and try to sleep. It's hard surface for sure, but that's a good thing because it won't let you get too deep in slumber, you got to get up to check that fire, add more wood, keep that temp at the sweet spot, constant check of hangings, you don't want them getting too crisp

(selling) in three to four days, all the sticks are covered in dried, shriveled leaves, one by one, you bring each woodsy fig-scented stick down from the rafters. Pile them and start cutting the strings. One trick - brace the tobacco stick in a window and clamp that pane down on it. Now you have both hands free to cut the string and strip off all the leaves. Peel off and sort all the dried pieces into three piles – good, medium, and junk. Good is crisp, but together. Medium is pliable but done. Junk is anything that is either still too stretchy or burnt to smithereens Once all the strings are cut and all the tobacco is sorted, use any softer leaves to wrap around the tops of bundles of the good and medium grades. Make them just as tight as you can, like a fist, then you're going to string them again back onto to the tobacco stick. Do this until each stick is fully packed with bundles ready for market. I'd save the junk pile of overcooked crumble and sell it end of the season whole for a little extra change. Someone always bought it. Nothing wasted.

Forgive them

My memories have grown sweet
writing to resolve troubles

we always hurt the ones we love
words we can't take back were spoken

I would have helped you a thousand
times over, but I didn't know how

I didn't have to be
in the room to hear you call me

bewilderment in your expression
I felt the helpless agony of it

long after, I felt your presence still
spirit unbound by walls or places

we were all taught ghosts
can jump and walk

I've heard you pound your cane
into the floorboards in night's hours

whisper through the hallway
we can't run from life

Love Letter to my Grandmothers

I will mend your veins, tangles of threads, shout
through inkberry and cobwebs, stir
the thrasher perched on palmetto, scatter
the sapsucker and swamp rabbit

I will don your folded apron, wrap
its supple second skin across my belly, husk
the pockets for your hymns, press smooth
as give of pine needles under bare feet

I will trace your embroidery with my fingertips, pry
off mason jar lids by front porch windows, remember
mottled salamander hiding under torn drapes, skitter
across glass pane, crescent moon claws tap *ti ti ti ti*

I will fix my heart to hold baptisms and prayers, quilt
them into lettered olive shell, catbird curve, cradle
the river of your blueprints in my palms, tremble
sand and salt chrysalis into unfurled swallowtail

your stone fruits, murmurs
                                        of mustard seeds
your sturdy psalter
                                        of soldering

Top Left, Grandmother; Top Right, Great-Grandmother; Bottom Left,
Mother; Bottom Right, Daughter/Author (held by Great-Grandmother)

A.M. Hayden is the Poet Laureate for Sinclair College and award-winning Professor of Humanities, Philosophy, and World Religions. She has received several pedagogy recognitions, including the League for Innovation Teaching Excellence Award (2020), and the Distinguished Faculty Scholars Award (2024). Her debut poetry collection, American Saunter, released December 2024 (FlowerSong Press). Old World Wings: Poems of Europe is forthcoming (Wild Ink Publishing).

A Pushcart Prize Nominee and River Heron Review Editors' Choice Winner, she lives on a windy little farm with her superhero partner, fierce daughters, and many rescue babies including their blind, three-legged, "angel in a dog suit" Vinny Valentine.

Hayden loves words, nature, and grits. This is her first chapbook.

Acknowledgments

First and always to God/Great Mystery, thank you is my prayer every single day. Abigail Wild and Wild Ink Publishing forever for believing in this book and the power of women's voices. Jason Blakely (Poetry is Life), J.R. Simons (Crisis Chronicles), Holly Brians Ragusa (Ohio Poetry Association President), and Sara Moore Wagner (Driftwood Press) for taking time out of their busy writers' lives to pen such beautiful blurbs for this little book. Angela Yuriko Smith, Furaha Henry-Jones, Jamey Coyote Dunham, my consistent poetry cheering section. Edward Vidaurre and FlowerSong Press for being the first to believe in me. Carlisle Lewis for your commitment to our family tree and Lilli-bug, you little sweet pea. Special thanks to Brenda and Randy Thompson, Wendy Rider, and Judy Hayden for sharing southern stories, laughter, and tears, which became the patches of this quilt. Jimmy, who my family adores more than me. Our daughters, forever and always, it is all for YOU, my big-time loves, to the moon and back, a bazillion times. Finally, for the readers of my first chapbook, thank you for spending time with my blessed half-southern heart.

www.ingramcontent.com/pod-product-compliance
Lightning Source LLC
Chambersburg PA
CBHW050857150626
46549CB00013B/3062